NEW
SUSTAINABLE
HOMES

NEW
SUSTAINABLE
HOMES

JAMES GRAYSON TRULOVE

COLLINS | DESIGN

An Imprint of HarperCollinsPublishers

NEW SUSTAINABLE HOMES

COPYRIGHT © 2006 BY COLLINS DESIGN AND JAMES GRAYSON TRULOVE

FIRST EDITION

FIRST PUBLISHED IN 2006 BY:
COLLINS DESIGN
AN IMPRINT OF HARPER COLLINS *PUBLISHERS*
10 EAST 53RD STREET
NEW YORK, NY 10022
TEL: (212) 207-7000
FAX: (212) 207-7654
COLLINSDESIGN@HARPERCOLLINS.COM
WWW.HARPERCOLLINS.COM

DISTRIBUTED THROUGHOUT THE WORLD BY:
HARPERCOLLINS*PUBLISHERS*
10 EAST 53RD STREET
NEW YORK, NY 10022
FAX: (212) 207-7654

PACKAGED BY:
GRAYSON PUBLISHING, LLC
JAMES G. TRULOVE, PUBLISHER
1250 28TH STREET NW
WASHINGTON, DC 20007
(202) 337-1380
JTRULOVE@AOL.COM

DESIGN: AGNIESZKA STACHOWICZ

LIBRARY OF CONGRESS CATALOGING-IN-PUBLICATION DATA

TRULOVE, JAMES GRAYSON.
  NEW SUSTAINABLE HOMES : DESIGNS FOR HEALTHY LIVING / JAMES GRAYSON
TRULOVE. -- 1ST ED.
        P. CM.
  ISBN-13: 978-0-06-113891-1
  ISBN-10: 0-06-113891-6
  1. SUSTAINABLE ARCHITECTURE. 2. ARCHITECTURE, DOMESTIC. 3.
ARCHITECTURE, MODERN--21ST CENTURY. 4. ARCHITECT-DESIGNED HOUSES. I.
TITLE.
  NA2542.36.T78 2006
  728'.37--DC22

2006015662

MANUFACTURED IN CHINA
FIRST PRINTING, 2006

PREVIOUS PAGES: Lengau Lodge, Photographer, Undine Prohl
RIGHT: Arbor House, Photographer, Greg Premru

50

60

96

108

120

164

CONTENTS

FOREWORD

Sustainable home design, renewable and recycled building materials, and renewable energy is no longer considered an exotic, utopian curiosity. It has, in the last few years, rapidly become a mainstream mandate among architects, home builders, and—most importantly—home buyers. Where once there were few resources to draw upon, now there are many. Not long ago, sustainable building materials were rare and costly, and many sustainable technologies were regarded as purely experimental and economically questionable. Not anymore. Soaring energy and building materials costs have leveled the playing field to the extent that passive solar heating, operable windows to capture summer breezes, and recycled lumber, stone, and steel for construction are primary topics for discussion when clients sit down with their architects to plan theirnew homes.

Amazingly, much that contributes to sustainable design is just common sense: providing adequate natural light to minimize daytime energy consumption; proper siting of the house and placement of windows to take advantage of nature's contribution to heating and cooling; and the use of native plant materials for landscaping, while capturing rainwater for irrigation. More sophisticated technologies, such as solar roof panels for electricity, and geothermal heating and cooling, are increasingly being requested by smart consumers who realize that, over time, the savings in energy costs will allow them to recover the additional costs.

Recycling is at the heart of any sustainable design undertaking, and the opportunity to use recycled materials in new home construction is almost limitless. From structural components and to insulation finished floors, the use of recycled lumber, steel, and even rags contributes not only to the well-being of the environment, but also to the bottom line.

Finally, sustainably designed homes are also healthier homes for the occupants. Synthetic building materials, over time, release volatile organic compounds (VOCs), some of which, like formaldehyde, are considered carcinogenic. Increasingly, manufacture's are offering low-VOC products, making the air inside the home cleaner and safer to breathe.

In *New Sustainable Homes,* a wide variety of projects are presented that explore the many ways sustainable principles can be applied to residential design. All are driven by the owners' desire to have not only a home that is beautifully designed and comfortable to live in, but also one that makes a positive contribution to the built environment.

LEFT: Solar panels cover the roof and wrap down the side of the Solar Umbrella House. RIGHT: A painted steel trellis provides pool-side shade from the hot Texas sun at the Spicewood home.

PROJECTS

SPICEWOOD

Situated on a bluff overlooking Lake Travis in Texas, the house is divided into a main residence with a large kitchen at its core and a guesthouse. The principal views are oriented toward the north, the view to the lake. As the house rises upward, the walls become more open, culminating in an office on the third floor with a 360-degree-view and an observation tower at the fourth level.

The exterior materials were selected to reflect the landscape: calico patterned limestone, light painted stucco, and Galvalume roofing: typical materials for the Texas Hill Country. The stone and stucco are coursed in strong horizontal bands, while the metal roofing folds into oversize gutters. Cypress wood stretches in a continuous plane from the 8-foot soffit overhangs to the second-floor ceilings. The same material wraps down the staircase and up to the third-floor office and fourth-level observation deck. At the highest point of the site, a 3,600-square-foot barn was constructed using a simple pre-engineered steel system.

SUSTAINABLE FEATURES:

The house is oriented with its long sides to the north and south, with the majority of the glazing on the north.

Deep overhangs protect the façade. A breezeway separates the garage from the house. The pool terrace between the house and guesthouse provides a welcome place to catch the prevailing winds.

The house can run entirely on rainwater that is collected from the barn roof into 20,000-gallon cisterns.

The mechanical system uses geothermal coils to displace heat into the ground, eliminating the need for noisy condensing units while conserving electricity use.

THIRD-FLOOR PLAN

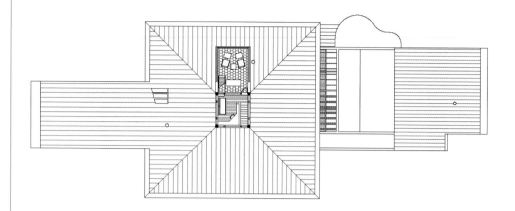

PREVIOUS PAGES: A view
of the side entry at dusk.
The house is positioned on a
bluff overlooking a lake. The
fourth-floor observation tower
provides 360-degree views.

SECOND-FLOOR PLAN

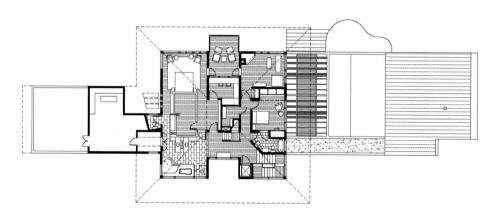

GROUND-FLOOR PLAN

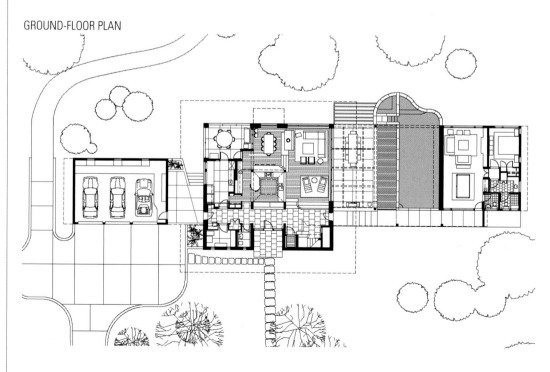

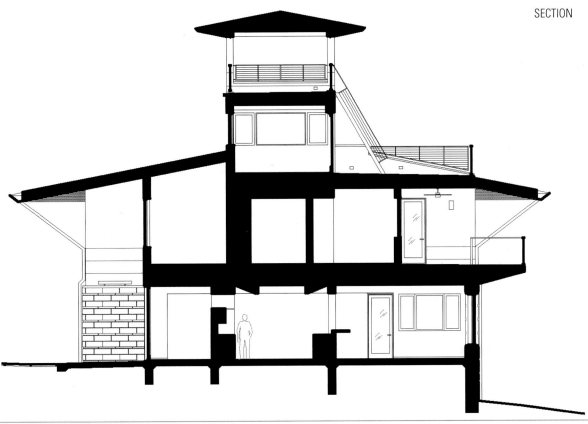

ABOVE AND LEFT: A painted steel trellis provides pool-side shade from the hot Texas sun. Dinners can enjoy the gentle, cooling winds in the evening.

ABOVE: The entry door
RIGHT: The living room opens
onto the pool terrace and is
bathed in natural light from
the extensive glazing on
three sides.

ABOVE LEFT: The second-floor landing
ABOVE RIGHT: The powder room
RIGHT: The master bathroom

ABOVE: The main entry. The exterior walls are constructed
of calico limestone and stucco.
LEFT: The side entry by the garages

CROWDER HOUSE

This 4,000-square-foot mountain residence, at an elevation of 9,300 feet, is located on a heavily wooded site in a natural clearing, which minimized the need for removing trees. Those that were removed were used for mulch and firewood for an EPA-approved woodstove in the main living area. The design is simple, yet dramatic. Two freestanding concrete boxes are connected by a second-level 70-foot-long "bar" that contains recreational space. The uphill box contains the garage on the first level and bedrooms on the second. The downhill box contains the kitchen and the living area with 22-foot glass walls on three sides. The master bedroom and bath are above. A custom staircase ascends from the living area to the bar.

Very low to no maintenance materials were used in construction, including flat and corrugated cement board panels on the exterior and on some interior walls. Equally important in this heavily wooded environment is the fact that all materials used for construction are non-combustible—metal studs were used for interior and exterior wall framing, steel joists and deck for floor structure, and structural steel and concrete for the building structure. The only combustible materials in the house are the furniture and wood stair treads.

SUSTAINABLE FEATURES:

Four-inch-thick concrete floors act as thermal mass for radiant heat gain. As a result, even on 15-degree days if the sun is shining, additional heat from the radiant floor system is not required. The virtually all-glass living area has double-pane low-E (low emmitance) glazing and is oriented primarily to the south, providing passive solar energy in the winter.

The house is not air conditioned. Operable windows and awning windows situated low in the large glass living room area allow cool air to enter. This air is pulled up the adjacent stair tower, which acts as a solar chimney, drawing hot air up and out of the house.

Landscaping consists of native trees and wildflowers, which require no irrigation except natural precipitation. Rocks and boulders gathered from the site were used for retaining and landscaping walls.

SECOND-FLOOR PLAN

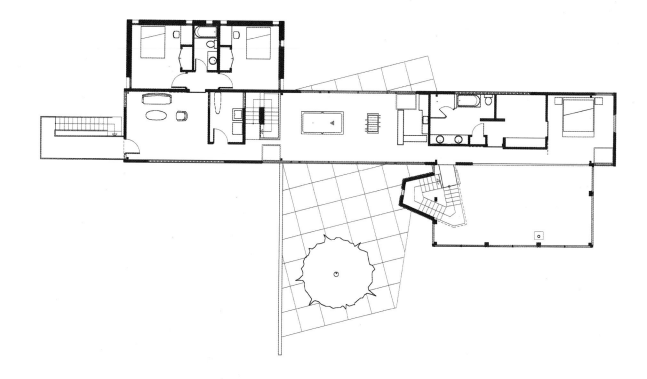

FIRST-FLOOR PLAN

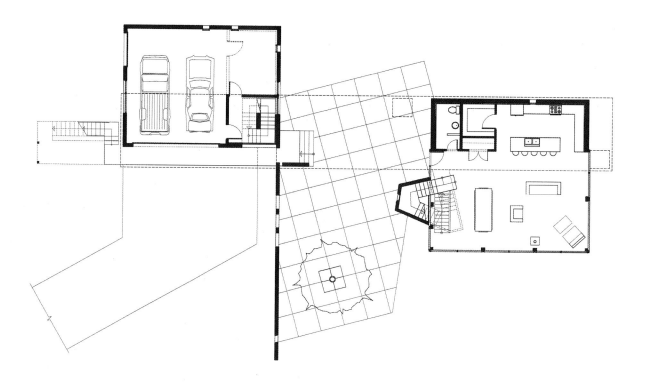

PREVIOUS PAGES: Two boxes rising from the earth are joined by a bar that acts as a bridge between them. The entirety is anchored by the vertical path of the stair tower, which operates as a stake in the ground around which the rest of the house flows.

SITE PLAN

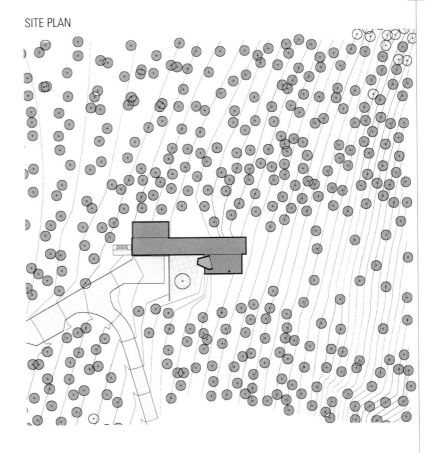

EAST ELEVATION

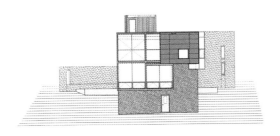

NORTH ELEVATION

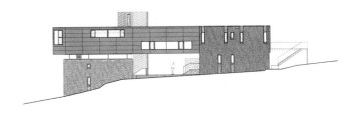

WEST ELEVATION

SOUTH ELEVATION

ABOVE AND LEFT: The second-level glass-and-concrete bar connects the two concrete boxes that serve as the foundation for the home.
FOLLOWING PAGES: Walls of glass in the living room bring nature indoors.

ABOVE: The kitchen is tucked under the bar. The stair tower
connects the living, dining, and kitchen areas to the bar.
LEFT: Detail of steel stair treads
RIGHT: A view of the master bedroom suite above the living area
FOLLOWING PAGES: A profile of the house at dusk reveals the
dramatic, modernist structure in all of its glory.

LENGAU LODGE

The Lengau Lodge is a private, family compound located on a wildlife preserve in northern South Africa. It consists of nine buildings, including four sleeping lodges, a master sleeping lodge, and a main lodge with a kitchen, dining area, and sitting area. The owners wanted a dwelling that had a close connection with the outdoors—that enabled exploration of native flora and fauna—and was suitable for large family gatherings. They built it as a home to be shared with friends and family from around the world.

The buildings are oriented toward the north to take advantage of the hills in the distance and the plains in the foreground, where animals tend to gather. The buildings are constructed from brick, with concrete bases, wooden roof timbers, and thatched roofing. To protect lodge occupants, the compound is surrounded by a solar-powered electric fence.

SUSTAINABLE FEATURES:

All bricks for the construction of the buildings locally manufactured and the timber came from sustainable sources. Structural timbers are pine that is locally plantation grown.

High ceilings and large gable end windows allow effective cross-ventilation. The gable windows are screened by large shutters that cut light while allowing transmission of air. The doors and windows were made of sustainably harvested Indonesian hardwood.

The thatching grass is a highly effective insulator. It was all locally sourced and is a sustainable roof material with a 15- to 25-year life span. Verandas on the north side of all buildings have planted roofs to shade and insulate the sunny side of the buildings.

The remote nature of the site requires that all sewage and water reticulation be dealt with on the site. Septic tanks overflow into aerobic rock filters and then into two constructed wetlands. This water is used for irrigation and is fed into a water hole for animals.

Landscape areas incorporate only plant materials that are locally endemic.

The buildings were sited on existing level pads wherever possible to reduce the amount of grading. All cut-and-fill work was carefully orchestrated to disturb vegetation as little as possible and to ensure no net import or export of soil.

PHOTOGRAPHER · UNDINE PRÖHL

MAIN LODGE FLOOR PLAN

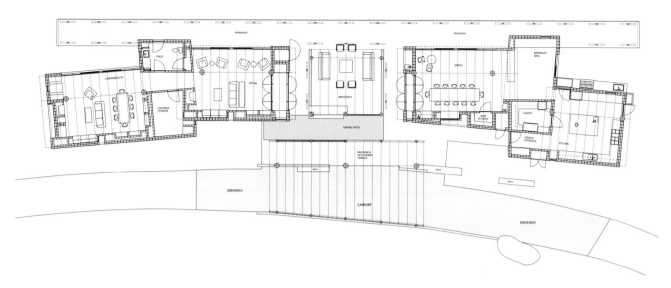

MASTER BEDROOM FLOOR PLAN

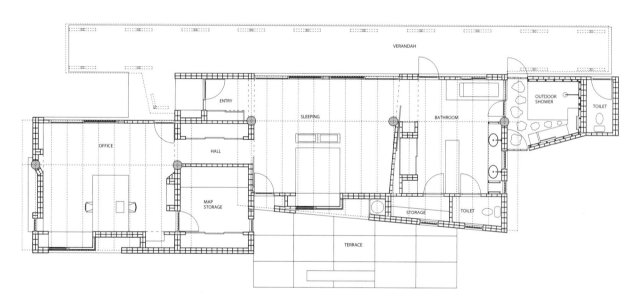

TYPICAL SLEEPING LODGE FLOOR PLAN

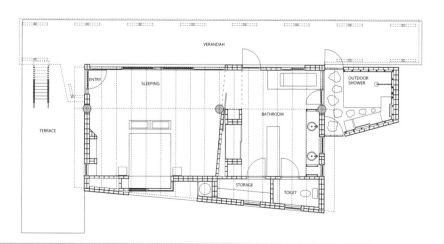

PREVIOUS PAGES: Exterior view of sleeping lodge number four with the roof of the veranda planted with local short grasses

NORTH ELEVATION SLEEPING LODGE

SOUTH ELEVATION SLEEPING LODGE

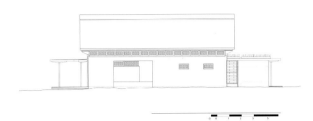

SECTION THROUGH MAIN LODGE AT COURTYARD

SITE PLAN

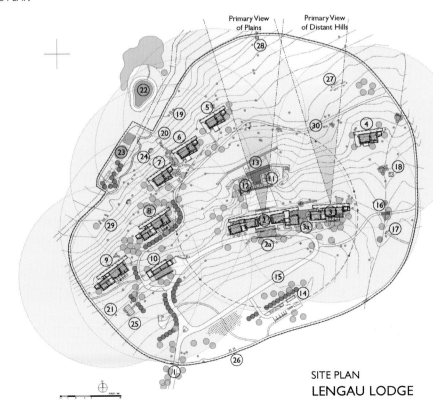

Primary View of Plains

Primary View of Distant Hills

SITE PLAN
LENGAU LODGE

KEY

1. Entry Gate
2. Main Lodge with Kitchen, Dining Sitting Room
2a. Porte Cochere
3. Master Sleeping Lodge
3a. Pond at Master Sleeping Lodge
4. Sleeping Lodge 1
5. Sleeping Lodge 2
6. Sleeping Lodge 3
7. Sleeping Lodge 4
8. Ranger Lodge
9. Staff Lodge
10. Workshops and Laundry Room
11. Pool with infinity edge, lawn and outdoor shower
12. Outdoor Kitchen and Dining
13. African Zen Garden
14. Vegetable Garden and Storage Area
15. Entry Drive
16. Concrete Dam
17. Perimeter Folly - Observation Bench / "Hammock"
18. Perimeter Folly - Rock Seating Platform
19. Perimeter Folly - Lounge Chair
20. Perimeter Folly - Game Hide
21. Rope Swings at Kudu-berry tree
22. Waterhole with overflow wallow for Warthogs
23. Water Filtration System and Wetlands
24. Perimeter Folly - Viewing Bench
25. Laundry Lines
26. Excercise Route - Step-up Curbs
27. Excercise Route - Push-up Pads
28. Excercise Route - Chin-up Bars
29. Excercise Route - Sit-up Benches
30. Golf Cart Path for Lodge access

I.

ABOVE: A view of the veranda and planted roof of sleeping lodge number four. Rock outcroppings were kept in place and the lawn areas are comprised of drought-resistant grass strains.

ABOVE: View across the water hole (filled with reclaimed water from the septic system) to sleeping lodge number three. Visible at the edge of the water hole is the electric fence and, at the base of the trees, a game blind.

LEFT: View of outdoor sitting area and gravel courtyard with the sitting room and family wing in the background. The floors are pigmented polished concrete slabs.

ABOVE: A view of the outdoor sitting area. The sitting room and family wing is on the right, and the dining and kitchen wing is on the left.

LEFT: The sitting room fireplace and connection to the family room
ABOVE: A detail of the exposed roof rafters and thatch. The
thatch was locally grown and has a useful life of 15 to 25 years.

ABOVE: A view of the interior of one of the sleeping lodges with the bathing and dressing area in the rear

RIGHT: A view of the bathroom and dressing area with the outdoor shower on the left. Water drains directly from these showers into adjacent planting areas. A clerestory window level separates the masonry base from the wood roof timbers above. These windows allows natural light to penetrate deeply into the buildings. The winter sun shines through these glazed areas into the rooms, heating the concrete floors and the interior of the thick masonry stenciled walls on the south side. As a result, the buildings require little or no additional heating from radiant wall panels.

ABOVE: The sleeping lodges. All paths, roadways, and site walls utilize local red oxidized sandstones, gravel as well as sand sedimentation from the same rock. Much of this material was found on the immediate site.

RIGHT: The game viewing platform outside of one of the sleeping lodges. The aloe "forest" and dry waterfall path to a game blind in the foreground. The aloe was grown on a neighboring farm.

WHITE RESIDENCE

Proper solar orientation for this 3,000-square-foot, three-story hillside residence was a key consideration in its design. All major spaces, including bedrooms, are oriented to the south, and all south-facing walls are composed almost entirely of operable windows and/or sliding glass doors, shaded by overhanging decks. It has an open staircase that connects all floors and acts as a thermal chimney to allow heat to rise from all levels of the house. The living spaces, along with kitchen and dining areas, are located on the upper floor, which has no attic. Instead, a curved roof creates an exhilarating sense of space, and ample natural light flows through the wall of windows. This level features commanding views of the Colorado River.

SUSTAINABLE FEATURES:

The cantilevered roof and the intermediate decks project over the south-facing windows, protecting them from midday sun in the summer while allowing sunlight to enter the house in the winter.

Windows were located to allow cross-ventilation and to admit the strong prevailing breezes from the river valley below. Low-E, double-pane vinyl windows were used throughout.

A single, high-efficiency mechanical fan system with a variable-speed motor allows the system to throttle back when full fan speed is not required. Each floor is zoned separately, but is on the same system, eliminating the need for redundant equipment. Ceiling fans are located in the living and dining areas and in all of the bedrooms.

Due to the zero-lot conditions of the site, almost no turf grass was used. Instead, native plants requiring littler water were specified.

Low-flush toilets and Energy Star appliances were installed.

A Galvalume standing seam metal roof reflects incident radiation before heat is transmitted. Kool-Ply radiant barrier plywood is used as a roof decking to reflect additional heat. The absence of attic space prevents unwanted heat gain and allows for higher ceilings on the upper floor.

PHOTOGRAPHER · GREG HURSLEY

SECOND-FLOOR PLAN

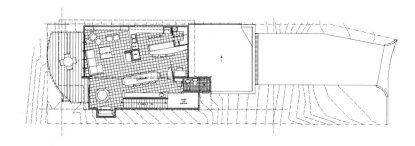

FIRST-FLOOR PLAN

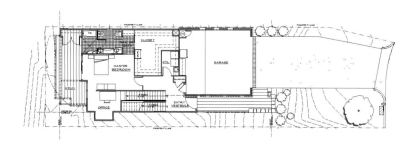

LOWER-FLOOR PLAN

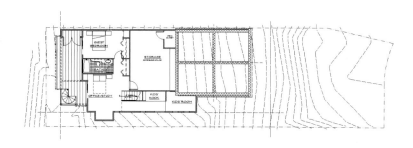

SITE PLAN

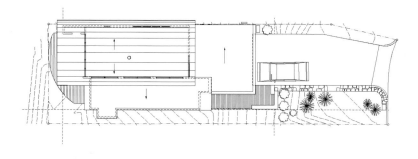

PREVIOUS PAGES: The property is a zero lot and the western wall of the house is built directly on the property line. Adjoining houses are only five feet apart. As a result, both the east and the west walls are usually shaded.

RIGHT: The living and dining areas are located on the top floor beneath a curved, cantilevered roof.

FAR LEFT: Flourescent cove lights were used to illuminate the interior of the curved roof above the kitchen, creating indirect ambient lighting at night. LEFT: Clerestory windows admit only morning sun while providing natural light throughout the day. As a result, little or no daytime electric lighting is required.

ABOVE: The upper-level living area enjoys spectacular views of the Colorado River.

RIGHT: The open stair connects all levels of the house and acts as a thermal chimney to allow heat to rise and exhaust through open windows on the south and east façades.

ABOVE LEFT: The master bathroom
ABOVE RIGHT: Low-flush toilets were
used in all of the bathrooms.
RIGHT: The entry is protected by a suspended canopy.

ARCHITECT · MARYANN THOMPSON

GEOTHERMAL RESIDENCE

The house is organized on the site to take advantage of the daily path of the sun. The kitchen faces east, while the living room and its terrace face west to take advantage of the setting sun. All rooms receive light on two sides. The combined living room, dining room, and kitchen area receives light on four sides through the use of a clerestory, enabling the sun to always be an ever changing presence in the main body of the house. The house was designed as a series of horizontal planes that terrace along the edge of a south-facing hill above a pond. The arrangement of the guest wing, main living spaces, and bedroom wing, which wrap along the hill's crest, is a response to the topography, solar orientations, and views beyond.

The interior is characterized by multiple planes of light entering into the house at a variety of levels. While the roof and floor planes establish the design parameters, the subtle articulations in the walls and windows provide close connections to the landscape and to the path of the sun.

SUSTAINABLE FEATURES:

The north façade is more insular, while the south façade opens the house to the site and the sun.

All rooms in the house receive cross-ventilation.

Large overhanging trellises modulate and dapple the intense summer sun —from the west and the south—at the living room and master bedrooms, while allowing the winter sun in.

Both the heating and the cooling systems are geothermal.

Sustainably harvested Honduran mahogany was used on the exterior and on the second-level floors.

Reclaimed quartersawn white oak was used for the first-level floors.

PHOTOGRAPHER · CHUCK CHOI

FIRST-FLOOR PLAN

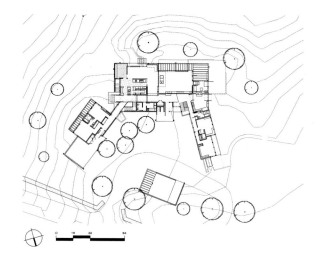

SECOND-FLOOR PLAN

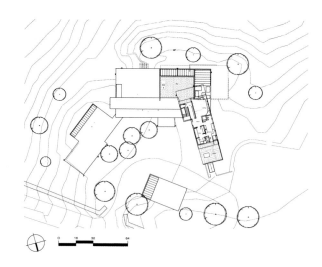

NORTH ELEVATION

PREVIOUS PAGES: The exterior of the house is sheathed in vertical, western red, cedar siding. The house was sited to preserve the large specimen trees on the gently sloping site.

RIGHT: The house was designed so that the interior flows to the outside terraces during the warmer months. The large overhanging western red cedar trellises modulate the summer sun while admitting the lower-angled winter sun's rays.

SITE PLAN

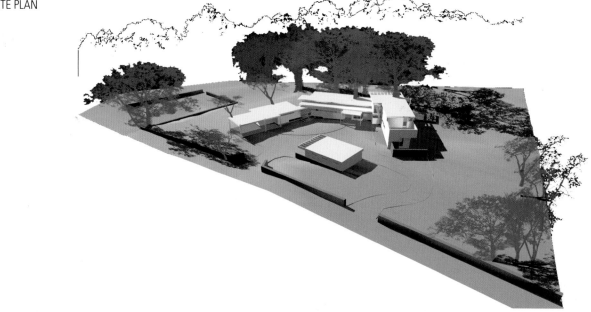

ABOVE: The horizontal planes of the floor and the roof extend beyond the large, glass openings, visually connecting the interior and exterior.
RIGHT: From the entry courtyard, the low profile of the house and the selective openings through the façade engage the visitor in a lively game of hide-and-reveal with the views that lie beyond.

ABOVE: Clerestory windows bring light from all sides into the living and dining areas.

RIGHT: Recycled, quartersawn white oak was used for the floor in the living room.

ABOVE: Natural light floods the first-floor living area, where all rooms enjoy cross-ventilation.
LEFT: The master bathroom is finished in Honduran mahogany and opens to an outdoor spa.

ABOVE: Honduran mahogany was also used for the master bedroom floor and all windows were made this wood.

LEFT: A guest bathroom is finished in gray slate and horizontal cedar boards.

FOLLOWING PAGES: A view of the south façade from the pond

ARCHITECT · OFFICE OF MOBILE DESIGN

SEATRAIN RESIDENCE

This home literally grows up from the land around it, engaging with and incorporating the industrial history of downtown Los Angeles through the use of found on-site materials. Grain trailers were transformed into a koi fishpond and a lap pool.

Large storage containers were used to create and separate the dwelling spaces within the house. Each storage container has its own individual function: one is the entertainment and library area; another is a dining room and office space overlooking the garden below; a third serves as the bathroom and laundry room; and the master bedroom occupies a fourth container, a visually dramatic protruding volume that wraps around the upper part of the house.

The recycled materials used to build this home were not just practical and cost effective, but they were assembled in such a way as to create a unique, dramatic architectural vocabulary. The innovative combination of recycled storage containers, grain trailers, steel, and glass resulted in a house that is highly sculptural, open, and L.A. modern.

SUSTAINABLE FEATURES:

This house was built entirely of recycled storage containers, grain trailers, steel, wood joists, and glass.

All principal building materials were found on-site, eliminating transportation costs.

The carpets are recycled floor coverings.

The site on which the project was built was, in essence, recycled, since it was previously used as an industrial site that was abandoned and then became an artists' colony.

Landscaping consists of low-maintenance, native plants

PREVIOUS PAGES: The large panels of recycled glass used throughout the house open up the space, allowing natural light to pour in while connecting the home to the surrounding artists' community.

BELOW: The house is located on the industrial site where the components used to construct it were located. A 12-foot-high steel plate fence wraps around the entire site.

SECOND FLOOR PLAN

FIRST FLOOR PLAN

SECTIONS

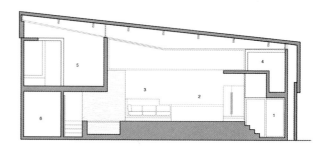

1/A5.1 section

1 utility room
2 kitchen/bar
3 lounge
4 dining
5 master bedroom
6 media room

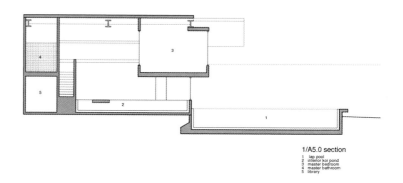

1/A5.0 section

1 lap pool
2 interior koi pond
3 master bedroom
4 master bathroom
5 library

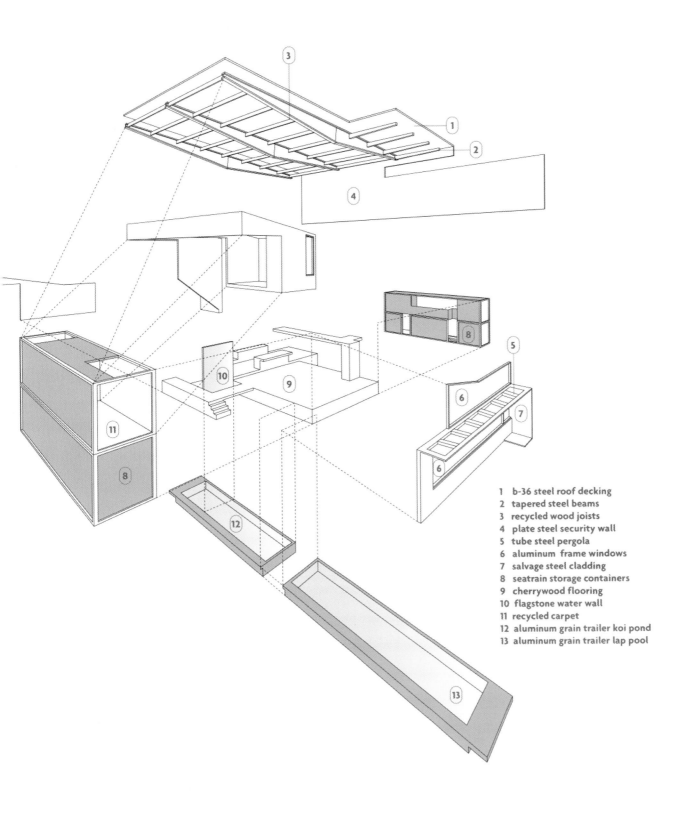

1 b-36 steel roof decking
2 tapered steel beams
3 recycled wood joists
4 plate steel security wall
5 tube steel pergola
6 aluminum frame windows
7 salvage steel cladding
8 seatrain storage containers
9 cherrywood flooring
10 flagstone water wall
11 recycled carpet
12 aluminum grain trailer koi pond
13 aluminum grain trailer lap pool

LEFT AND ABOVE: A koi pond made from a recycled grain trailer was inserted into the native landscape. The low-maintenance plantings require little water.

LEFT: The living room overlooks a lush garden transformed from an industrial site.

ABOVE: The interior lap pool is also constructed from a grain trailer. The master bedroom, located in its own shipping container, was cantilevered above.

ABOVE AND LEFT: Warm, calm green and yellow hues highlight
the dynamic interplay of materials and forms such as the
contrast of corrugated metals, industrial containers, and
exposed wooden beams.
FOLLOWING PAGES: One container accommodates a generous
walk-in shower, while another serves as the master bedroom.

EDGEMOOR HOUSE

From a design standpoint, the goal for this project was to create a home that would fit comfortably within a traditional postwar neighborhood, while addressing the client's desire for a more contemporary house. The existing structure was torn down to the foundation walls and the first-floor deck became the footprint for the new house.

From the street, the gable roofs establish a dialogue with the traditional houses within the neighborhood. The cast limestone brise-soleil, or sunscreen, recalls the scale of front porches found on the nearby houses and marks the axis of the entry. Inside, a gallery runs the length of the house, dividing the kitchen and dining room from the guestroom and family room. The modern face of the house is expressed in an outdoor room overlooking the rear of the site.

SUSTAINABLE FEATURES:

Minimal maintenance required for exterior materials

Vertical-loop geothermal-fed radiant heating and chilled coil water cooling system

Cork flooring and FSC (Forest Stewardship Council) certified wood flooring

Veneer cabinets on non-formaldehyde-based paneling

Icynene high-density insulation

Low-E argon gas aluminum windows

The new house was built on the existing foundation walls of the previous structure that occupied this site.

FIRST-FLOOR PLAN

SECOND-FLOOR PLAN

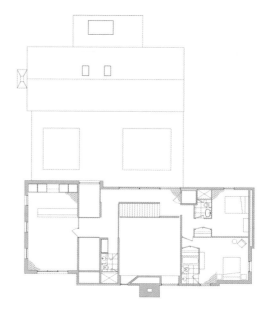

PREVIOUS PAGES AND RIGHT: The juxtaposition of shapes and textures—the stuccoed rear volume, the cast limestone brise-soleil, and the Butler stone volumes—create an abstract composition. BELOW: Window detail

SITE PLAN

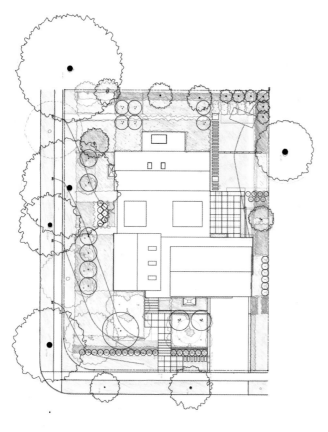

ABOVE LEFT: East façade
ABOVE: North façade
LEFT: West façade

BELOW: A view of the entry. The entry procession ends at the double-height master suite volume.

RIGHT: An animated stairway overlooking the family room leads up to a catwalk between the guestrooms and a bridge to the media room.

ABOVE: A view of the kitchen
from the brise-soleil
RIGHT: The two-story living room

ABOVE: The kitchen as seen from the dining area
RIGHT: Clerestory windows bring natural light into the high
ceilings of the kitchen.

ARCHITECT · PUGH + SCARPA

SOLAR UMBRELLA

A bold solar umbrella addition transformed the architects' existing 650-square-foot bungalow into a 1,900- square-foot residence equipped for responsible living in the 21st century. The solar panels wrap around the south elevation and roof of the new addition, becoming the defining formal expression of the residence. These panels protect the body of the building from thermal heat gain by screening large portionsof the structure from direct exposure to the intense southern California sun. Rather than deflecting sunlight, this state-of-the-art solar skin absorbs and transforms the sunlight into usable energy, providing 95-percent of the building's electric load through 89 amorphous silicon solar panels.

Recycled, renewable, and high-performance materials and products were specified throughout. For the existing house, new insulation was blown into the walls, and roof, and batting insulation was provided under the floor. Hardscape and landscape treatments were employed for both their aesthetic and their actual impact on the land.

SUSTAINABLE FEATURES:

Homosote, an acoustical panel made from recycled newspaper, was used as a finish material for custom cabinets. Oriented strand board (OSB), composed of leftover wood chips compressed together with high-strength adhesive, was used as a primary flooring material along with concrete. Also, recycled steel panels, solar-powered in-floor radiant heating, high-efficiency appliances and fixtures, and low volatile organic compound (VOC) paint were specified.

A storm water retention system retains 80 percent of roof storm water on-site. The landscaping is native and drought-tolerant planting with a substantial amount of gravel to allow water to percolate into the ground. A drip irrigation system with seasonal adjustments was installed. The roof storm water is collected in a large scupper, which is directly above an underground retention basin and allows a majority of the roof water to be retained on-site.

Three solar hot water panels are used to preheat the domestic hot water before it gets to the gas-fired hot water heater and the swimming pool.

PHOTOGRAPHER · MARVIN RAND

SECOND-FLOOR PLAN

SECOND FLOOR PLAN

PREVIOUS PAGES, BELOW, AND RIGHT: A view of the solar umbrella that covers the wall of the south elevation and the roof of the new addition at the rear of the lot. The swimming pool is heated with water from solar panels.

FIRST-FLOOR PLAN

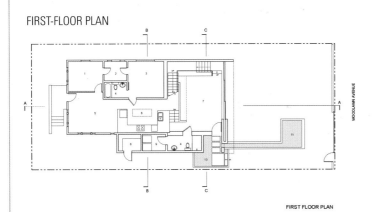

FIRST FLOOR PLAN

1 STUDY   9 LAUNDRY
2 CLOSET   10 FISH POND
3 BEDROOM   11 JACUZZI
4 BATH   12 MASTER BEDROOM
5 DINING ROOM   13 MASTER BATHROOM
6 KITCHEN   14 PATIO
7 UTILITY CLOSET   15 ROOF BELOW
8 UTILITY CLOSET

SCALE IN FEET

SECTION A

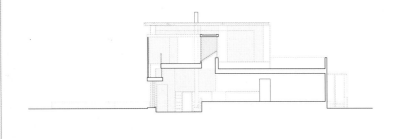

SECTION C   SECTION D

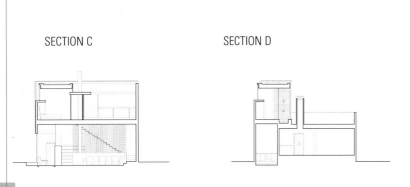

FAR LEFT, LEFT, AND ABOVE: Operable windows and a perforated-steel stair are strategically placed so that as hot air rises, it passes through and out of the house. The rooms are kept cool with a combination of window placement for cross-ventilation; double-glazed, krypton-filled, low-E windows with stainless steel spacers; and recycled insulation that boosts the thermal value of the wall to 75 percent above a conventional wood frame wall construction.

LEFT: The major materials used were concrete with 50 percent
fly-ash content, and recycled mild steel that was rusted and
then sealed. Wood products were constructed from composite
recycled materials for cabinets, flooring, and structure. High-
efficiency appliances were used in the kitchen.

LEFT AND ABOVE: The master suite on the second level is located directly above the new living area. The bedroom opens onto a deep covered patio that overlooks the garden. This patio extends the bedroom area outdoors, creating the sensation of a sleeping loft exposed to the exterior.

ABOVE: The entry door is made of recycled steel.

RIGHT: An existing garage was torn down and replaced with a smaller carport. Permeable gravel was used instead of concrete for the driveway, allowing water to percolate into the ground. The stucco used on the exterior has an integral colored pigment so that painting is never required. All concrete forming materials and 20 percent of the framing material were from reclaimed sources.

ROBBS RUN

The architect's clients for this project were a young couple, with two small children, who wanted a house that incorporated principles of sustainability throughout the design, including saving specimen oak and elm trees studded throughout the irregular lot where an existing house had been demolished.

The resulting three-story house is split into two essentially equal rectangular volumes connected by a glass slot, which provides circulation and also floods the interior of the house with light. The lower floor contains storage, a study, and garages, and is anchored to the site by its concrete block form. The upper two stores appear to float above the street, giving the sensation of living in a tree house.

SUSTAINABLE FEATURES:

A 1,200-gallon rainwater collection cistern is used to provide plant irrigation.

Salvaged stone from a former house on the lot was reused to build the fireplace and retaining walls.

High-performance spray insulation was used for the entire exterior envelope of the house, including the sealed attic space.

The high-efficiency water-cooled air-conditioning system utilizes an evaporative condenser, a variation of a cooling tower.

Solar photovoltaic roof panels generate 3 kilowatts of electricity.

75 percent of the interior cabinets were made from VOC-free compressed wheat board.

Landscaping utilizes native plants with low water consumption. The house was sited to protect specimen trees.

PHOTOGRAPHER · GREG HURSLEY

SECOND-FLOOR PLAN

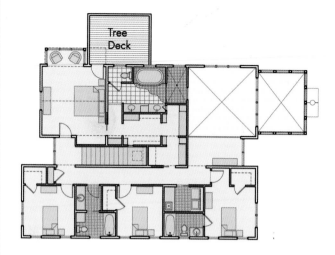

Tree
Deck

FIRST-FLOOR PLAN

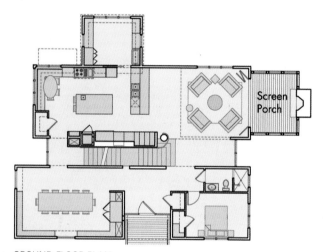

Screen
Porch

GROUND-FLOOR PLAN

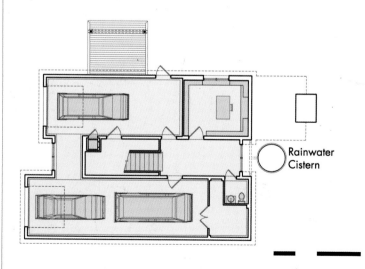

Rainwater
Cistern

PREVIOUS PAGES: The design of the house consists of two three-story rectangular volumes connected by a glass wall that brings natural light deep into the house.
BELOW RIGHT: The architect designed the house so that mature specimen oaks and elms on the site were preserved.

SITE PLAN

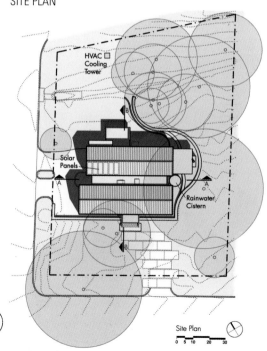

HVAC
Cooling
Tower

Solar
Panels

Rainwater
Cistern

Site Plan
0 5 10   20   30

SECTION A

SECTION B

FAR LEFT: A view of the
childrens' playroom
cantilevered from the
side of the house
LEFT: A generous screened
porch also features a
fireplace that was made
from stone recycled from a
previous house on the site.

ABOVE AND RIGHT: Large double doors open to join the two-story family room with the screened porch, bringing fresh air into the house.

ABOVE: A major programmatic requirement was to provide ample wall space for the owners' growing art collection. The solution was to construct walls along the circulation spine of the house. RIGHT: Running behind these walls is the staircase to the second-floor bedrooms.

LEFT: The master bathroom
ABOVE: Child's room

ARCHITECT · D'ARCY JONES DESIGN

ISLAND HOUSE

This home, perched on a steep bank overlooking a protected ocean harbor on Vancouver Island's south coast, was designed as a vacation house for an extended family. Summers spent at an original cabin on-site provided the clients with intimate knowledge of the breezes, light, and vegetation, which informed all aspects of the new house's design. The project consists of a 2,400-square-foot main house with an 800-square-foot office and bedroom wing. Three of the house's bedrooms were designed for sleeping and work: wall beds fold down from built-in office shelving. The guest bedroom and office wing is connected to the main house with a covered breezeway, providing acoustic separation. A generous living and dining space is flanked by a kitchen, pantry, laundry, and bath. An oversize Rumford fireplace is the focal point of the main living space, contrasting with the small adjacent inglenook.

Exterior and interior materials were chosen for longevity, and all building materials were locally grown and sourced. Douglas fir was used for the post-and-beam construction, with tongue-and-groove decking above. Cedar benches and the morning deck were built from standard construction lumber. Bleached cedar was used as an exterior siding fillin select areas. The entry features an adze-carved Douglas fir door. All custom shelving in the house was made from vertical-grain Douglas fir veneer plywood. The limited areas of white- painted drywall hide mechanical equipment and a built-in sound system.

SUSTAINABLE FEATURES:

The property's microclimate is very dry, with long hot summers. Large overhangs were tuned to annual sun angles, preventing overheating during the summer. Low winter sun penetrates deep into the plan because the simple mono-pitch roof rises to the west.

The thick concrete walls successfully function as a thermal mass in cool and hot seasons. Summer cooling is aided by cross-ventilation from carefully placed low-E glass operable windows to catch onshore and offshore breezes.

Rainwater from the gutter that runs the entire width of the house is directed down chain leaders to an underground cistern for irrigation of the all-native plants on the site.

During construction, an established orchard, a vegetable garden, and existing trees were preserved.

FLOOR PLAN

PREVIOUS PAGES AND RIGHT: The house was constructed of poured-in-place concrete walls with full-height aluminum and wood windows and doors. The low-E glass—used in conjunction with deep eaves, operable windows, and the thermal mass of the solid (and insulated) concrete walls—eliminates the need for air-conditioning.

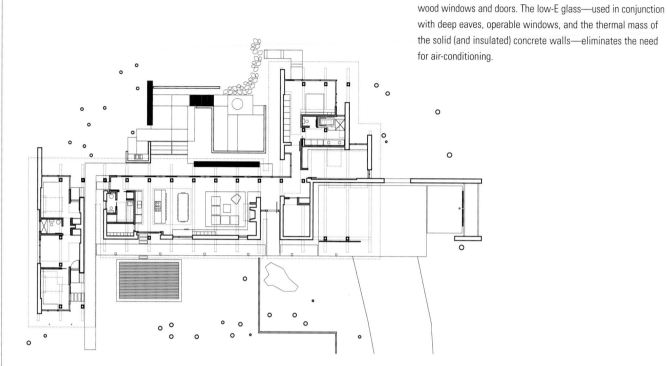

SITE PLAN

SECTIONS

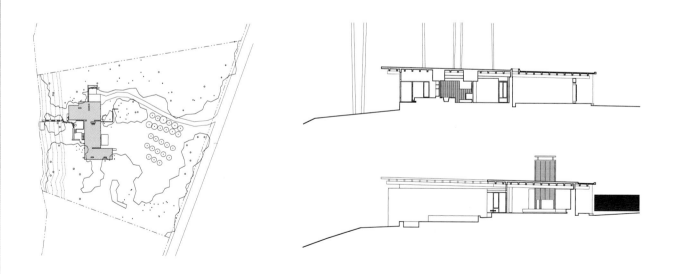

LEFT: Rainwater from the gutters runs down the chain into an underground cistern. FAR RIGHT: Polished exterior concrete slabs appear to extend the living areas to the exterior terraces.

LEFT AND ABOVE: The polished concrete floors were embedded with radiant heating. Locally grown Douglas fir was used for the post-and-beam construction. The floor-to-ceiling windows and doors allow the open living area to spill out onto the terraces.

LEFT: The thick concrete walls function as thermal mass in cool and warm seasons, significantly reducing energy consumption.
FAR RIGHT: Much of the activity at this house takes place outside, overlooking the ocean harbor.

ARCHITECT · MARYANN THOMPSON

THE GREEN HOUSE

This simple and refined contemporary residence on a densely wooded lot is surrounded by grand, neocolonial homes in a conventional suburban development. The clients, one an environmental lawyer, wanted an environmentally sensitive and sustainable design executed within a limited budget. The deliberately straightforward scheme—a simple box form adorned with a single trellis and an asymmetrical roofline—is a direct response to the clients, who suggested that the house express the attitude of "benign neglect." It was constructed of low-maintenance and naturally occurring materials, and fits comfortably and unobtrusively within its over-five-acre wooded site.

Within the tight footprint, the 3,000-square-foot residence offers ample public spaces for entertaining and cozy private spaces—all of which are connected, visually or physically, to the existing woodland.

SUSTAINABLE FEATURES:

Solar panels and pellet stoves reduce energy consumption.

Recycled materials for construction and finishing were used when possible, and included reclaimed hardwood cabinets, recycled glass tiles, and a roofing system of recycled tires.

Windows on three sides of the living spaces assure adequate cross-ventilation and eliminate the need for mechanical air-conditioning. In the winter, numerous windows on the southern elevation provide passive solar heating.

The asymmetrical roofline of the southern elevation shields the upstairs bedrooms against intense summer sun.

A trellis provides shade without obstructing light.

PHOTOGRAPHER · CHUCK MEYER

SECOND FLOOR PLAN

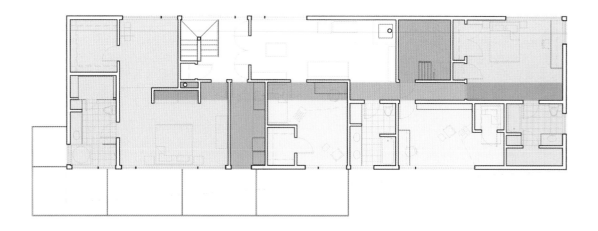

FIRST FLOOR PLAN

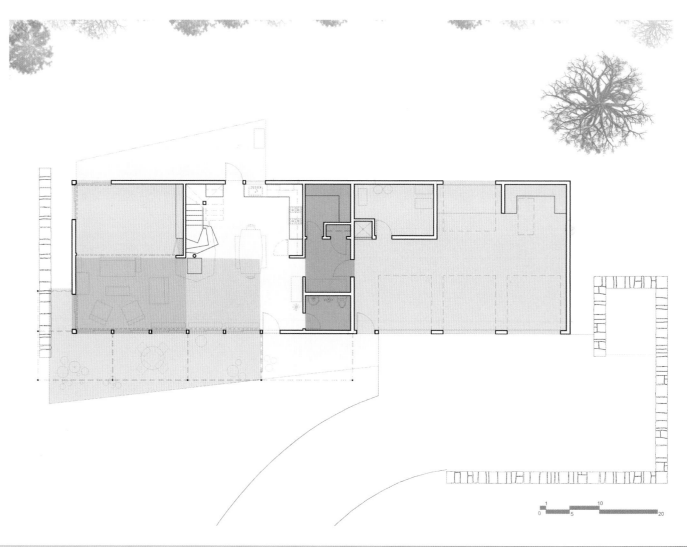

PREVIOUS PAGES: Sliding doors adjacent to the living and dining spaces preserve unobstructed views of the landscape and promote an indoor/outdoor lifestyle. The asymmetrical roofline shades the patio at mid-day and screens the main living spaces against harsh light. The exterior building materials include Hardy Plank siding, a sustainable composite.

SITE PLAN

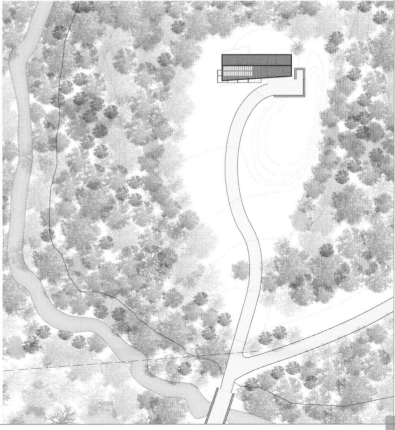

ABOVE: In the kitchen, appliances were selected for Energy Star ratings. The refrigerator, by Kenmore, is the most efficient on the market, while the gas range is the only product available that does not require an external electrical source. The stained concrete floor is warmed by radiant floor heating.

RIGHT: Lit from beneath, the open stair of FSC-Certified Maple and covered steel cable is a sculptural element in the house's oetherwise simple and direct design. The sconces fabricated from 100 percent recycled acrylic and mimic frosted glass, while the fixtures themselves are efficient compact flourescents.

LEFT: An expanse of sliding doors on the south elevation invite
sunlight, warmth, and ample ventilation into the body of the scheme.
ABOVE: The L-shaped living and dining area opens to the landscape
on four sides through sliding doors. The sun's movement throughout
the day creates ever-changing light patterns across the concrete
floor. The partition door, at right, creates a sound proof media and
music room without a permananet enclosure.
FOLLOWING PAGES: At night, the house appears to hover just
above the landscape. The exterior light fixtures, approved by the
International Dark-Sky Association, are down lights which do not
contribute to night time light pollution.

TANNER RESIDENCE

The clients for this modern home built in the spirit of the "cracker" homes of central Florida's early pioneers wanted an environmentally friendly dwelling that was economical to build and, maintain. Large, mature oak trees which where, left undisturbed on the site protect the home from Florida's harsh afternoon sun. Designed to maximize cross-ventilation, the home is only 20 feet wide and is raised off the ground on concrete columns. A cost-effective structural system was utilized that incorporated many prefabricated elements.

SUSTAINABLE FEATURES:

The house is raised off the ground to encourage natural ventilation and promote material longevity by reducing the opportunity for rot and termite damage. Because of the minimal amount of excavation required for the foundation, the natural slope of the landscape was left undisturbed.

The narrow 20-foot width of the house promotes cross-ventilation both through the home and underneath it.

The highly reflective Galvalume roof and siding reduce solar heat gain.

Low-E insulated glass was used for all of the windows, which have aluminum frames.

Bamboo flooring was used in all principal rooms. Ipe, a sustainable hardwood, was used for decking and window louvers.

On-demand hot water heaters reduce energy costs.

PHOTOGRAPHER · MAX STRANG

FLOOR PLAN

PREVIOUS PAGES: The house is raised off the ground to promote ventilation and to minimize excavation of the site.

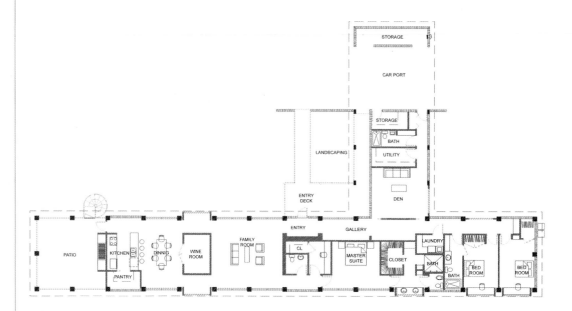

SECTIONS

CONSTRUCTION DETAILS

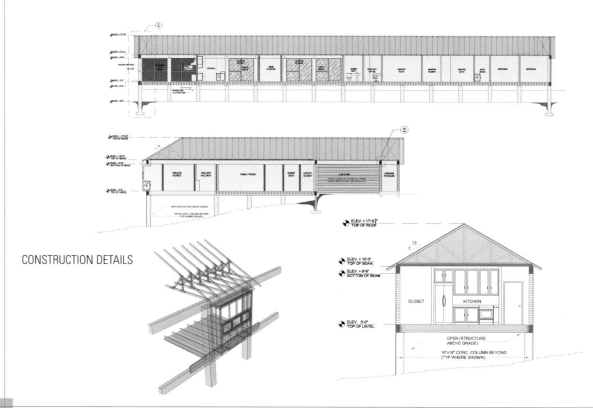

NORTH ELEVATION

WEST ELEVATION

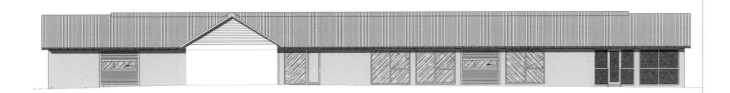

SOUTH ELEVATION

EAST ELEVATION

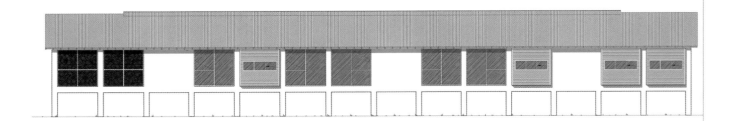

ABOVE: The long east elevation, which is only 20-feet wide provides unimpeded views of a nearby lake from the house's hillside perch.
LEFT: Entry
RIGHT: Large oak trees provide welcome shade from the hot Florida sun.

LEFT: A gallery with bamboo floors runs the length of the house, connecting all of the major rooms. Paintings by Florida artist Jim Draper recall the native landscaping.

LEFT: The kitchen and dining area
ABOVE: The master bedroom

LEFT: A view from the lake at dusk

ARBOR HOUSE

This 800-square-foot guesthouse, whose design was inspired by the vineyards, wooden boats, and seines that are common on Martha's Vineyard where it is located, is used year-round and is entirely heated and cooled without the use of fossil fuels. This was achieved through the careful siting of the house, the placement of windows, and the materials used in its construction. In the winter, heat from the sun's low angle is absorbed in the concrete and stone of the walls and floor, while in the summer, when the sun's angle is higher, deep roof overhangs provide shade.

Outside, an 800-square-foot courtyard extends the living area. This outdoor space is defined by a grape arbor that, when mature, will provide additional shade for the house.

SUSTAINABLE FEATURES:

The house was designed for passive solar heating and cooling with no supplementary mechanical systems. Additional heat is provided by two high-efficiency wood-burning stoves with timber collected from the 7-acre site.

The structure was oriented on an east/west axis for optimum southern exposure with the critical ratio of 1 square foot of solar glazing to 7 square feet of thermal mass.

Insulation and air filtration barriers exceed state standards.

The ratio of 3 square feet to 1 square foot of operable windows oriented toward prevailing (southwesterly) breezes induces air movement.

Deep overhangs and sun shading devices on the southern and western façades assist in cooling the house in the summer months.

In-line duct fans either redirect or exhaust heat that has risen to the ceiling, depending on the season.

A tankless hot water heater provides water on demand rather than consuming energy when not in use.

FLOOR PLAN/SITE PLAN

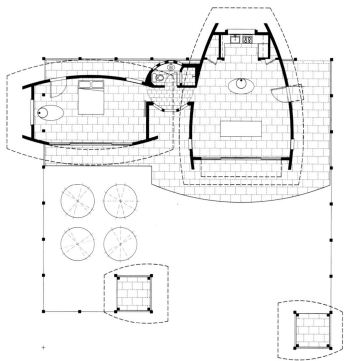

PREVIOUS PAGES: The curvilinear roof was made of lead-coated copper that is long lasting and maintenance free. In keeping with the nautical motif of the house, the patterns of the shingles recall a seiner, a common fishing net.

BELOW: The south elevation has large windows to catch the low-angled sun's rays in the winter and deep roof overhangs to shade the house from the steeper-angled sun in the summer.

Plan

Scale

0'   5'   10'

NORTH-SOUTH SECTION

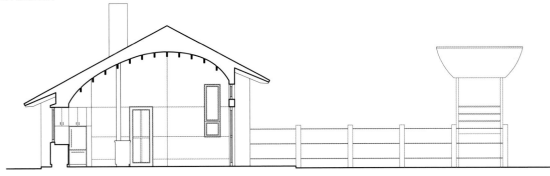

NORTH ELEVATION

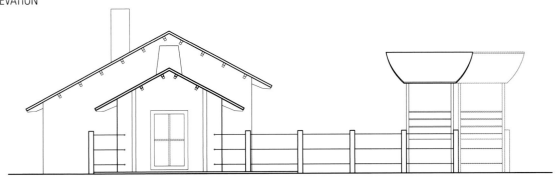

EAST-WEST SECTION

SOUTH ELEVATION

Scale
0'   5'   10'

ABOVE: The bedroom wing

RIGHT: The kitchen/living wing; a courtyard doubles the livable space of the house. It is bordered by a grape arbor that will provide additional shade when it matures.

LEFT: All furnishings for the house were custom designed by the architect. The table trestle was modeled on an eel.
ABOVE: One of two high-efficiency woodstoves is located in the kitchen/dining area. The slate floors were laid on a concrete subfloor and make up most of the house's thermal mass.

LEFT AND RIGHT: The custom beds create a room within a room when the surrounding curtains are closed. The second woodstove is located in this space.
FOLLOWING PAGES: The exterior courtyard is flanked by two raised platforms.

BASAS RESIDENCE

This 2,350-square-foot slab-on-grade house rests on the back of a low ridge on 21 acres in rural Virginia. An existing logging road was utilized as the driveway to minimize site disturbance. The house was designed with an unobstructed internal circulation path between the public and private spaces to accommodate handicapped accessibility. Sinks and a workstation were set at a height to accommodate a wheelchair. There is a 5-foot turning radius in the kitchen corner, hallways are 4 feet wide, pocket doors were used instead of swinging doors, and drawers and shelves were used in the kitchen instead of swinging cabinets.

The high shed roof facing southeast captures daylight and direct solar gain. The lower side creates an intimate setting anchored by a stone hearth and chimney made of salvaged stone. The stepped plan creates exterior spaces adjacent to the center of the house.

SUSTAINABLE FEATURES:

The house is orientated to maximize passive solar gain.

Locally sawn poplar siding and white oak trees that were removed during construction were milled and used as exterior posts for the porch on the north side of the house. Salvaged stone from an earlier building was used for the fireplace. Maple for custom cabinets, which were built by a local cabinetmaker, came from trees harvested nearby.

BioBased soy foam was used for exterior insulation, and recycled denim from old blue jeans provided insulation inside for sound attenuation.

High-performance, metal-clad, low-E, argon-filled windows were used, and sill plates are borate-treated Enviro-Safe Plus, containing no heavy metals or arsenic.
The paint throughout the home is low in volatile organic compounds (VOC).

Energy Star appliances were selected for the kitchen, and a high-efficiency heat pump was installed for heating and cooling.

SOUTH ELEVATION

SECTION

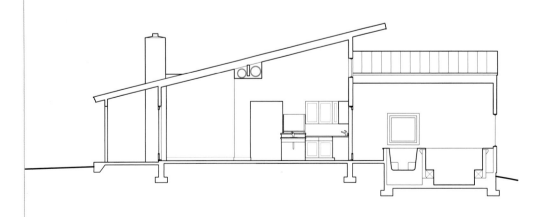

PREVIOUS PAGES AND BELOW: A view of the entry and terrace. Large expanses of metal-clad, argon windows on the south façade maximize passive solar gain. The hydrotherapy pool at the end of the terrace is adjacent to the master bedroom and bath.

ABOVE AND RIGHT: The kitchen and living area benefit from large, south-facing windows and a clerestory. A sink in the kitchen is positioned at wheelchair height. Cabinets were constructed by local craftsmen from maple trees harvested nearby.

LEFT: The living room fireplace was constructed from stone originally used in an 18th-century dwelling. Pocket doors were used throughout the house for easier accessibility.

ABOVE: The master bedroom. The floors are integrally colored concrete with radiant heat.
ABOVE RIGHT: The master bathroom connects to the indoor pool.
RIGHT: The master bathroom
FOLLOWING PAGES: A view of the southeast elevation at dusk